# THE 6 YOUNG TITANS

*And the Race to Stop the Wacky Scientist*

Sam Deen

Book design by Joseph Reece
Cover design by Shumaila Khan

ISBN – Paperback : 9781395865702

First Edition: October 2024

# CONTENTS

# 1

## MEET THE TITANS

The morning sun rose over London, wrapping the city in a sunny glow. In the Titan Residence, the family was a hive of activity. The six siblings were getting ready for the day, each in their own unique way.

The eldest Faisal was up and ready. He was tall and lean with a confident posture and sharp, intelligent gaze. His sleek attire reflected his knack for learning.

His brain was fast-paced, which allowed him to take in information at a super-fast speed. But he always respected elders, especially his parents, so he tried to slow his speech when talking with them – well, he TRIED!

"Faisal, can you please slow down a bit? I can barely keep up with you," his mother said, her hands on her hips.

"Sorry, Mum, I've just got so much to say!" Faisal replied, grinning.

He ran past her, his mind already racing through the day's schedule. Faisal grabbed an apple on his way out of the kitchen and knocked on Taiba's door.

They were practically twins, just a year apart. So, naturally, he knew getting her teddy bear army ready took extra time. He knocked on her door, entered, and sat on a beanbag in her bedroom.

Inside, Taiba was organising her magical teddy bears. Her sparkling eyes and happy smile made everyone feel cheerful. One thing about Taiba was that she was super organized, as it helped her have a clear mind. She packed her school bag and zipped it shut. The zip had a glittery teddy bear hanging from it.

"Come on, bears, time to spread some love!" she said as she prepared her cart filled with all her teddy bears in it.

The bears blinked and stretched as if waking from a nap.

Taiba's bears had a special power: they came to life when someone needed help. She had a whole teddy bear army ready to give hugs and spread kindness! She named them things like Cuddles, Snuggles, and Mr. Fluffykins. Each had the unique ability to come alive when someone needed a hug or a helping paw. And they were always ready for an adventure.

As she arranged them, Taiba noticed one of her

favourite bears, Mr. Fluffykins, looking a bit sleepy.

"Come on, Mr. Fluffykins! We've got work to do!" she giggled, giving him a gentle pat.

Mr. Fluffykins, with a sleepy yawn, blinked one button eye open. "But Teeba" (a nickname they have for her), he mumbled in a tiny voice, "it's nap time!"

Taiba giggled again.

"We can't nap now! There are hugs to be given, smiles to be shared! Remember, sleepyheads can't help people!"

Suddenly, a muffled cry came from the next room.

"Taiba, my hair is trying to grab everything again!"

Taiba bit her lip to hold back a laugh. Mr. Fluffykins sighed dramatically.

"Oh dear, Saba and her out-of-control hair... one day, it'll take over the world!" he declared with a tiny frown, his voice barely a whisper.

Just then, Saba burst into the room, looking like

she'd been wrestling a hurricane. Her long, curly locks grabbed at everything in sight.

"Not today, hair," she muttered, finally managing to tie her hair back with a golden scrunchie. The hair gave a reluctant twitch but stayed put—for now. Saba's hair was not just long and curly; it was alive! It could grow and stretch to grab things or people. One time, it even saved a kitten stuck in a tree. But today, it was more interested in some kind of hair Olympics!

As she finished, her hair tried to sneak out a strand to grab a nearby book.

"Nope, you stay put!" she scolded, giving it a little flick. Speaking of staying put, there was someone who never did—Abdullah!

Even at 7 in the morning, this sibling was in the garage, tinkering with the family's old car. His cargo pants were filled with tools, and his hoodie sleeves were rolled up. Abdullah was only a year and a half younger than Saba, but his baby face and childish smile made him look much younger.

"Just a little more," he said, tightening a bolt. The car sputtered to life, and Abdullah grinned.

"Perfect." He gave the bus a proud pat, accidentally triggering the horn, which blared loudly. He jumped back, startled, and then laughed.

"Maybe a little less perfect."

Abdullah touched the big car, and it shrank to a pocket-sized toy car. He slipped it into the front pocket of his trousers. Ahh... how much he loved doing that!

He loved anything with wheels, in fact. Cars, bikes, scooters—you name it, Abdullah could drive it. He even drove a tractor once, much to their neighbour's surprise. His favourite trick was shrinking vehicles to pocket-size, making him the ultimate driver-on-the-go.

"Abdullah, the school bus is here!" called his dad from the kitchen.

"Coming, Dad!" Abdullah answered back. He

picked up his bag and headed for the school bus, looking forward to seeing his friends at school.

Zaynab was not as pleased, unfortunately. She was rehearsing her speech for poetry class when she heard the bus horn. Zaynab's voice could be both a blessing and a whammy. It was powerful enough to stop bad guys in their tracks, but sometimes it got her into trouble—like the time she accidentally shattered all the glass in the school's trophy case.

Yes, her super screech could break stuff. So, she always had to be extra, extra, EXTRA careful. Always. But sometimes (or maybe lots of times) she forgot. Like she did now...

"Oh no!" she cried before putting her hand on her mouth, realizing her mistake.

Sure enough, everyone stopped, covered their ears, and ducked. Thank God the bus had plastic windows! The bus driver, looking like a grumpy cloud, lost control for a moment as her screech pierced through his ears.

This was the third broken headlight this week... she really had to control her voice. She made a sorry face as the bus driver observed the broken headlights of his vehicle.

Faisal and Saba stepped onto the school bus, with Taiba at the back, pulling along her cart of teddy bears. Zaynab was still inside, panicking.

Abdullah, the nice big brother he was, popped out from the school bus again. He knew Zaynab had a big poetry reading in class and was feeling jittery. He went to find her, even if it meant being late himself.

Zaynab took a deep breath and started reciting her poem. She recited,

"O, wind, if winter comes, can spring be far behind?" Her speech was so loud it rattled the windows and sent pigeons flying in all directions.

She winced.

"Sorry."

"Maybe keep it down a tiny bit, honey," her mum suggested with a gentle smile as she came downstairs.

"Okay, Mum, I'll try," Zaynab promised, taking another deep breath and starting over, this time much softer.

Even though she was small, her big eyes showed exactly how she felt. With her bag strapped tight on her back, she marched toward the door, ready to rock her poetry reading.

Before leaving, though, she caught Baby Salman on his changing mat, drooling and smiling—the youngest of the lot. Thick slobber dripped from his chin, trapping their grumpy cat, Sharpie, in a slimy mess.

Baby Salman was the youngest and couldn't yet talk, but his drool was something special! It turned into super sticky slime that could trap anything—or anyone. It was both gross and handy. Sharpie, however, wasn't a fan.

Speaking of whom, Zaynab had named the cat "Sharpie" herself due to a peculiar marking on the side of his body that resembled someone using a marker pen to scribble on him. Faisal, being Faisal, thought the name was perfect because the cat was sharp, just like him.

Salman's giggles filled the house, breaking Zaynab out of her thoughts. Sharpie's unhappy meows were mixed somewhere there, too.

"Salman!" Zaynab cried, rushing to free the cat. Mum was the first to arrive, distracting Salman while she gently lifted Sharpie from the sticky goo.

"All right, little man," Dad said, scooping up Salman.

"Let's keep the drool to a minimum today."

After saving the cat and securing Salman, the two rushed to join their siblings on the bus.

Each of them had a special talent which led to certain... surprises. And today would be no exception.

# 2

## THE TITANS ASSEMBLE

The bell rang, and school started with lots of excitement and a bit of chaos. The Titans were all set, and Faisal was already ahead of the game.

Speeding through his history presentation, words tumbled out like a runaway train.

"Therefore, the Mesopotamian agricultural revolution, with its use of irrigation techniques, undoubtedly..."

Mr. Jonah, his history teacher, blinked rapidly, his expression a mixture of awe and mild terror. The rest of the class looked like a troupe of confused goldfish.

Faisal loved this part. Seeing their faces was priceless!

He finished his presentation and returned to his seat at the far corner with a satisfied smile. His friend, Adam, leaned over and whispered,

"Dude, I think you broke Mr. Jonah."

Faisal chuckled.

"Just wait until you see my science project. It's going to make Mr. Jonah question everything he knows about physics!"

Adam raised an eyebrow.

"Are you sure he can handle it? Last time, he looked like he'd seen a ghost when you explained how magnets work."

Faisal grinned mischievously.

"Exactly! This time, I'm bringing in a potato clock!"

Adam shook his head with a laugh.

"Well, let's hope he survives the day!"

Faisal nodded, still grinning.

"Oh, he'll survive."

Faisal glanced out the window as the presentations went on, spotting Taiba sitting on a school bench across the playground. It was her sports class, but she was surrounded by her teddy bears. Her tales always ended with a happy-ever-after, and her bears loved every minute of it.

"And so once again, the day is saved thanks to the brave little bear," Taiba announced, concluding yet another story.

Taiba's teddy bears had bright button eyes that sparkled with joy as she read them a story about a brave little bear who saved the day with kindness. Her radiant smile only played the part of an enchanting storyteller. A nearby captivated toddler clapped his chubby hands and giggled with delight.

As she finished, one of the teddy bears, Mr. Cuddles, turned to Taiba and asked,

"Can we hear another story, Teeba?"

"Of course, Mr. Cuddles!" Taiba replied, hugging the bear tightly.

Close by, Saba was walking to class. She was nose-deep in her book when she yelped in surprise. Her hair had snatched a freshly baked doughnut from the cafeteria bakery as she passed through there to get to her class. A big man with a flour-dusted moustache, probably the school cook, chased her hair through the halls, waving a dough roller after it.

Saba couldn't help but giggle as her hair held the doughnut high above the baker's reach.

"Sorry, Mr. Baker! It's not me, it's my hair!" Saba's laughter could be heard in the school parking lot—a sound that reached the ears of Abdullah, tinkering under the hood of the sputtering school bus parked there. But his focus was elsewhere.

"Fuel line's clogged, faulty spark plugs... easy fix," he muttered to himself.

Within minutes, the engine purred back to life, earning him grateful cheers from the impatient children inside. Abdullah loved the sound of a well-tuned engine—it was about the sweetest thing to his ears.

"Thanks, Abdullah!" the bus driver called out as the bus drove away.

"No problem!" Abdullah waved back, his face beaming with satisfaction.

"Gotta join Zaynab, though," he muttered, wiping his grease-stained hands on his overalls.

"Poetry class is going to start soon."

Across the schoolyard, Zaynab was determined to keep her volume under control this time.

"If I can just keep it at a reasonable level," she whispered to herself.

She began reciting her poem softly,

"O, wind, if winter comes, can spring be far

behind?" This time, only a few glasses trembled, and she breathed a sigh of relief. Zaynab's teacher gave her a thumbs-up, and she grinned with all her teeth showing.

***

By midday, the siblings met for lunch under their favourite big oak tree. They chatted and swapped stories about their morning. Suddenly, Faisal's sharp ears picked up a bit of a news report from a nearby radio from the school teachers' lounge.

"Strange occurrences have been reported across London," the announcer said. "Witnesses claim to have seen unusual lights and heard bizarre sounds in several locations. Traffic lights gone haywire, puddles of green goo appearing on sidewalks, and reports of washing machines...talking!"

The siblings exchanged worried glances.

Faisal turned on his special mission phone,

tapping into a web of information only he could understand.

Taiba hugged her teddy bear tight, worry in her eyes.

Saba twirled a strand of her hair, wondering if it had anything to do with the weird happenings.

Abdullah tapped his foot, ready to spring into action.

Zaynab swallowed, feeling nervous.

The air went quieter than a library at nap time. There was a nervous tension... and then,

"Sounds like a job for the Titans, doesn't it?" Faisal grinned.

Everyone gasped. At that very moment, even though their heads were spinning, a giant superhero firecracker went off inside them all. The six kids huddled close under the tree and simply looked at each other. No big speeches, just a quick nod – they knew what to do!

It was time for the Titans to assemble!

# 3

## THE FIRST CLUE

The Titans' secret headquarters was upstairs of their house, hidden away in what looked like a super dusty attic. It was stuffed with books 'older than dinosaurs,' as Faisal would call them.

But this attic was way more than meets the

eye. The walls were covered with shiny gadgets that blinked and buzzed, and the floor was a jumble of maps. These maps showed everywhere they'd already explored on daring missions and all the places they dreamed of going next. It was like the Titans' imagination had come alive! And it was wild.

Suddenly, the door burst open with a bang.

In a blur of motion, Faisal barged inside the door where his siblings already sat—his sleeves rolled up to his elbows and white sneakers squeaking as he paced around. As soon as he came in, his words tumbled faster than a squirrel on espresso.

"Titans, assemble! London's in a colossal kerfuffle of epic proportions, and I, through the meticulous application of my advanced deductive reasoning skills, have managed to crack the code with the precision of a laser!"

Taiba peeked out from behind Mr. Cuddles, who wobbled dangerously, its single-button eye struggling to keep track of Faisal's rapid explanation.

"Whoa there, Einstein! You talk faster than Mr. Fluffykins chasing a butterfly on a sugar high! Our brains can't keep up!"

Abdullah, with pockets overflowing with gadgets, played with a miniature drone that buzzed wildly around his head.

"Yeah, slow down, brother. And tell me you didn't download another dictionary?"

Faisal skidded to a halt, his brow furrowed in seriousness.

"This is a situation of monumental gravity, guys! London has descended into utter pandemonium! Green goop oozes from buildings like a particularly sluggish and, frankly, unhygienic waterfall, traffic lights belt out off-key opera at rush hour, inflicting auditory torture upon the unsuspecting populace, and washing machines gossip about dirty socks in the spin cycle, a blatant invasion of privacy for undergarments everywhere!" He paused, taking a dramatic breath.

"It all points to one culprit – the disappearance of Dr. Wonky, I mean, the esteemed Dr. Quirky, the mad scientist!"

Saba raised an eyebrow. Her long, curly strands twitched as if sensing something fishy.

"Talking washing machines, Faisal? I mean, that can't all be true! Did you perhaps bump your head a little? Let me check for a second."

"Dr. Quirky's inventions are wackier than wack, sis!" Abdullah quipped before Saba could get up, his drone narrowly missing a vase and causing a minor disaster.

"I mean, who can forget the Shakespeare-toast toaster? After that, anything is possible."

Zaynab gave a hearty laugh at that. The room was soundproof, and there was nothing a loud shriek could break here... except for human ears. Everyone groaned and covered their ears. But Zaynab couldn't resist and grabbed a nearby spatula, holding it up like a microphone.

"In the fair kitchen, where we lay our bread. From ancient grudge breaks to new mutiny. Where civil crumb makes civil crusts unspread," she proclaimed dramatically, mimicking the voice of a toaster reciting Shakespeare. Her silly attempt at a pretend sonnet made her laugh even harder.

Abdullah joined in the laughter.

"To toast, or not to toast, that is the bread-ly question!"

Before they could continue with more toaster-themed theatrics, Saba interrupted their fun with a serious tone,

"Enough guys, please. Faisal, please continue! What's the brilliant plan to crack this nutty case?"

And just like that, their attention returned to the matter at hand.

His fingers flying across a holographic keyboard that pulsed with colourful light, Faisal grinned.

"According to my super-sleuthing skills," he announced, his voice dropping dramatically,

"Dr. Quirky vanished from his lab in North London. If anyone can untangle this gooey, glitchy mess, it's definitely him!"

"Hold on a second," Taiba said, looking puzzled. "How do you know all this?"

Faisal's eyes sparkled with excitement.

"Elementary, my dear Taiba! Utilizing my unparalleled proficiency in deciphering encrypted data streams, coupled with my extensive repository of knowledge on anomalous phenomena, I was able to deduce the precise location of the aforementioned scientist through a meticulous process of elimination and cross-referencing various sources. Simple as pie, really!"

His siblings' heads spun as they tried to keep up with his rapid-fire speech.

"Uh, what?" Zaynab asked, shaking her head to clear the confusion.

Faisal grinned and slowed down just a bit.

"Google!"

"Dr. Quirky's lab is in North London. If we find him, we can solve this mystery!" he continued eagerly, his eyes shining with excitement.

With that said, they all scurried out of the attic, which was an adventure in itself. They kept a hidden trapdoor behind a giant painting of a sleepy owl wearing funny glasses. After a bit of wobbling and near-slipping, they descended the creaky ladder.

Finally bursting out the front door, they tumbled onto the lawn in a jumble of arms and legs. And with a battle cry, the Titans scrambled into Abdullah's car, but not before it transformed into a sleek silver car with a magical tap from Abdullah's hand.

"Buckle up, London, because the Titans are on the case!" Zaynab shouted as they drove off, breaking the car windows.

# 4

## THE MYSTERIOUS LAB

With hearts pounding, the Titan siblings stepped out of Abdullah's gadget car, which he then tapped to make the size of a mouse and put in his pocket.

"North London... home to upperclassmen, clever kids, and, apparently, missing scientists," Faisal wondered out loud.

The Titans stood outside the huge building housing Dr. Quirky's lab. Taking a deep inhale, they snuck inside, tiptoeing past a grumpy security guard who looked like he hadn't slept since the invention of the internet. – 1983

From inside, it looked less like a scientific haven and more like a toddler's party gone bonkers. Beakers overflowed with suspicious liquids that bubbled like overexcited soda. Wires wound across the floor like angry snakes, and gadgets buzzed with a weird energy.

Abdullah whipped out his high-tech gadget and scanned the room like a detective.

"Whoa, these readings are off the charts!" Abdullah announced with a worried frown.

"There's definitely some serious science stuff going on here, not your average school lab experiment, that's for sure."

Faisal was deep in Dr. Quirky's notes, which looked more like scribbles made by Baby Salman with a marker. He couldn't make out most of it. Before he could answer, Saba's hair twitched and pointed towards a dusty old desk.

"Hey, what's that?" she asked, her hair reaching out to touch a bubbling test tube. The teddy bears, too, saw a playground of scientific discovery. Taiba, however, wasn't as thrilled.

Soon, Captain Smartypants was head-down in the basket of paperwork when he found a dusty scroll. As he proudly presented his find, his teddy legs snagged on a loose wire, crash-landing straight into Mr. Cuddles, who managed to get his head stuck in a particularly stinky beaker.

And in a heroic attempt to free his friend, Mr. Fluffykins accidentally knocked over a vial of glowing green liquid. The liquid splashed onto Mr. Giggles, causing him to inflate like a giant, fluffy balloon.

The lab erupted in chaos.

The glowing liquid, apparently allergic to boredom, reacted with everything it touched. One beaker exploded, showering Zaynab's clothes in smelly goo. Another flask launched Abdullah's mini-backpack into a wild frenzy, narrowly missing Saba, who was busy trying to untangle her hair from a particularly aggressive wind-up monkey toy.

The domino effect continued, with glass shattering, bubbling potions spraying around, and a robotic arm, awakened by the commotion, swatting poor Mr. Pookie Bear across the room.

The lab now resembled a scene from a particularly messy food fight.

Thinking fast, Saba used her hair to grab a fire extinguisher and blast a hole in Mr. Giggles, deflating him with a satisfying whoosh. Finally catching his breath after dodging a flying wrench, Faisal scanned the room wearing goggles he hadn't worn before he came in.

"Whoa! This place is cluttered!"

Taiba, looking at the wreckage, whistled sharply.

"Enough teddy bears! We need to find clues, not create them!"

Through the smoke, they saw Mr. Giggles, now glowing an alarming shade of radioactive green but thankfully unharmed. Captain Smartypants, a second before collapsing on the ground, held out the scroll. Its edges were slightly charred but still readable.

Carefully unfolding it, they saw a few lines scribbled in Dr. Quirky's messy handwriting:

*"The next hint you seek, in a park you'll peek,*
*where danger might wait or a life you might save.*
*But beware! For the name of this park,*
*it's where fun abounds, with a twist that's around."*

"It's the..." Faisal squinted at the message on the screen.

"Ooh! It's gotta be Teddy Bear Park!" Taiba bounced, her voice bright with excitement.

"Think about it, teddy bears and fun, duh!"

Saba giggled.

"Nah, it's probably a hair salon. You know, where they twirl your hair and make it all fancy-schmancy?"

Zaynab huffed.

"Clearly, it's a poetry club! Words get twisted and rhymed, see? Fun with poems!"

Abdullah rolled his eyes.

"Too easy, sis. Come on, think harder."

Baby Salman gurgled and drooled, adding his own commentary.

Saba's hair whipped around excitedly and pointed at a giant map on the wall. Faisal scratched his head, the gears in his brain churning.

"Maybe it's the Royal Observatory Planetarium? Space is fun," he suggested hopefully.

Everyone stared at him with blank expressions.

Out of nowhere, Sharpie yowled, making them all jump. Zaynab couldn't help laughing.

"Sharpie, where did you come from, you furry

mystery of a cat?"

The cool cat sashayed over and plopped himself right on the map, his paw pointing directly at a spot labelled 'Round Park.'

Zaynab gasped. "Look! Round Park!"

Faisal's eyes widened.

"Round Park... or maybe... Circular Park?"

Taiba's eyes sparkled like stars.

"What if it's Merry-go-round Park? Fun, twists, and saving the day? It all fits!"

Everyone stared at Taiba, jaws on the floor.

Faisal grinned from ear to ear.

"Taiba, you might just be a genius!"

Abdullah pumped his fist.

"Then let's go find this Merry-go-round Park!"

"Hold on," Faisal said, his grin fading as he looked at the machine that was making a beeping, flashing racket.

"We might have a bigger problem first..."

Suddenly, Saba's hair twitched again, this time

wrapping itself around a lever like it was trying to hold on for dear life. To make matters worse, the sleepy security guard burst through the door.

"What in the world are you little gremlins doing up here?" he boomed.

The Titans exchanged panicked glances. Looks like their secret location wasn't so secret anymore.

# 5

## A TWIST IN THE TALE

Faisal whispered, his voice barely audible,

"Quick! To the secret exit!"

Taiba whispered back, equally panicked,

"Wait, there's a secret exit?"

Faisal gave a know-it-all expression.

"Yeah, follow me!"

The siblings ran towards a hidden door disguised as a bookshelf. Saba's hair yanked the lever as they squeezed through the door, revealing a super cool slide that whooshed them down into a dark tunnel.

They landed in a heap in the alleyway, gasping for air.

"Whoa, that was close!" Faisal exclaimed.

Mr. Giggles, a little worse for wear, still radiated a faint green glow while all the bears gathered around him, concerned.

Mr. Giggles wobbled.

"To the Merry-go-round Park!" he declared only to face-plant into the grass with a surprised.

"Oopsie!"

Abdullah shook his head, amused. Reaching into his pocket, he pulled out the tiny car once again. He gave it a double tap, and the car grew bigger and bigger until they could all pile in. And then, they were off.

\*\*\*

Upon arrival, they noticed the park was a maze of slides, swings, and suspicious-looking bushes.

They searched for the Merry-go-round like squirrels on a nut hunt, getting lost five times in the process. Just as Zaynab was about to declare a mutiny for ice cream, a loud scream split the air.

There, clinging to a tree branch that swayed as unsteadily as Mr. Giggles, was a little boy—his voice as loud as Zaynab's, if not louder. The grown-ups circled the tree, all passing poor tips like "Don't look down" or "Hold on tight!"

Faisal couldn't hold the sight anymore.

"Action time, Titans!" he declared.

But before they could spring into action, the ground beneath them trembled. A dwarf purple monster with mismatched socks lumbered into view. Its eyes were like googly, wiggly eyeballs, and it wore a party hat. The adults screamed, and the children cried.

The monster gurgled, moving towards the tree. The boy screamed even louder.

"Oh no!" cried Taiba.

"What are we going to do?"

Zaynab, however, wasn't scared. She puffed out her chest and marched right up to the monster.

"Stop right there, you monster! Why are you picking on that little boy?"

The monster blinked its googly eyes.

"Me? Pick on him? No way! I just wanted to help him."

Everyone stared.

*Help him? Help him how?*

The monster reached down and fumbled behind a tiny, floppy ear. He pulled out a giant, wonky cake. Unfortunately, the cake was upside down and covered in what looked suspiciously like mashed broccoli.

The boy peeked down from the tree.

"Uh...," he mumbled.

"I mean, I did pray for a cake..."

"Oh yes, he did! I heard it from under the ground. It's where I live!" The monster looked down at his mismatched socks.

"Maybe I should have gotten him a new pair of socks, too."

Zaynab tilted her head and looked at the monster. It didn't seem so scary anymore. In fact, it seemed kind of adorable.

Zaynab, always open to new friendships, offered before it could turn his back and leave,

"Wait! Are you hungry?"

The monster paused.

"Hungry? Yes, very."

She quickly rummaged through his backpack and pulled out a homemade energy bar.

"Here, take this."

The monster sniffed it, then devoured it in one

bite.

"Delicious!" it exclaimed.

"No one has ever given me food before."

Saba's hair, sensing an opportunity, wrapped around the monster gently.

"Would you like to hear a poem?" Zaynab offered.

The monster's fierce expression softened.

"A poem? For me?"

Zaynab nodded and began:

*"In a park so round, where fun is found,*
*A monster waits, misunderstood, not bound.*
*With a kind heart and a hunger profound,*
*A friend in disguise, in this merry-go-round."*

The monster's eyes filled with happy tears.

"No one has ever been *this* kind to me before. Thank you."

The Titans smiled.

"Kindness is everything," Zaynab said.

"Now, why don't we all help you give the boy a proper cake?"

The monster's droopy face lit up.

"Really? You would do that?"

"Of course!" boomed Zaynab.

"We're the Titans, and we help people... even misunderstood monsters with mismatched socks!"

The monster looked like he had finally found the last piece of a jigsaw puzzle.

"I will help you find what you seek. I was told some superheroes would be coming looking for clues. I'm guessing you're them?"

"Indeed, we are! Can you help us? Were you instructed to do so?" Faisal asked.

"Of course not! I was asked to chase you away. But you were brave, and you were kind. Now, I am your enemy turned ally. I shall now take you to the clue you need to help save London!" The monster replied.

"By the way, my name is Earthecho."

So, with Earthecho's guidance, the Titans found the next clue, tucked away safely beneath a hollow tree. They thanked their new friend and promised to visit her again.

Faisal said,

"You know, kindness really can change everything."

As they left Merry-go-round Park, the parents showered their thanks on the "talking teddy bears," Faisal unfolded the map. His eyes widened. It was a detailed sketch of an old, abandoned warehouse on the city's outskirts. Could this be linked to Dr. Quirky and the nationwide chaos?

"Thank you, Titans," the child's mother said with a smile.

"You saved the day!"

The Titans shared a secret smile. Saving the day was one thing, but maybe, just maybe, this map was the key to saving the entire city.

# 6

## HAIR-RAISING
## ADVENTURE

The Titans raced through the busy streets of London in Abdullah's super cool transforming car. Baby Salman giggled as the car sped past double-decker buses and red telephone booths. Taiba's magical teddy bears peeked out from the windows, waving at shocked pedestrians.

"Almost there, guys!" Abdullah yelled over the engine's roar, steering towards a spooky old warehouse from their secret map.

*CRASH!* The car stuttered and stalled, not before it crashed into a tree.

"Uh-oh, out of gas!" Abdullah groaned.

"No worries, brother. We can walk from here," Taiba said with a smile.

"Besides, the teddies could use the exercise!" These teddy bears weren't exactly Olympic athletes, but they enjoyed a good waddle.

Mr. Grumbles, the grumpy one, grumbled extra loudly about the whole walking thing.

The Titans hopped out of the car and began walking towards the eerie warehouse. Its rusty doors creaked in the wind like a rusty swing set, and cobwebs decorated the broken windows.

"Eek! Are we really going in there?" Mr. Giggles squeaked, his colour finally returning.

Saba, with her perceptive hair, grinned mischievously.

"No worries, Mr. Giggles! My hair will help us

sneak in without anyone noticing."

"If anyone's even in there," Mr. Grumbles sighed.

Saba's hair slithered out of the car window with a flick of her head, weaving through the air like a curious snake. It stealthily wrapped around the door handle and gently pulled it open. The Titans slipped inside, tiptoeing past stacks of dusty crates and creaky machinery.

Inside, it was dark and musty, with mysterious shadows playing tricks on their eyes.

"I can't see a thing!" Zaynab whispered loudly, her powerful voice booming across the empty warehouse.

"Don't worry, Zaynab," Faisal reassured her, his intellect kicking into high gear.

"I've got a flashlight in my backpack." He rummaged around and soon produced a tiny flashlight that barely lit up their path.

Suddenly, Saba's hair, which had been scouting

ahead, gave a startled yelp.

"Ouch! My hair's stuck on something!"

The Titans rushed over to find Saba's hair tangled in a mess around a stack of old bicycle tyres. They couldn't help but hold back their giggles at the sight of her hair wrapped around the tyres like that.

"Come on, Saba! Wiggle your head gently," Taiba advised, trying not to laugh too loud.

Faisal tried to be helpful, but *oops!* He tripped over a loose board and landed with a *thump*. He sputtered and coughed, looking as grumpy as Mr. Grumbles. Before he could utter a word, a loud creaking noise from above startled them all.

A rusty trapdoor in the ceiling swung open with a creak, and down tumbled a swarm of glowing butterflies! They fluttered and flew in the air, creating a breathtaking spectacle. Unfortunately, they saw Saba's hair as their perfect nesting place.

Saba's eyes widened at the sight of all the butterflies flying towards her and wriggling their way in between her hair knots and gaps in the bicycle tyres.

"NOOOOO!!! YUCK, YUCK, YUCK!!! GROSSSSSSS!!!!" Saba squealed and yelped, flapping her hands everywhere. "GET THEM OFF MEEEEE!!"

Everyone burst into a fit of laughter as they shooed off all the butterflies, making sure they flew elsewhere and left Saba's hair alone.

As the last butterfly settled elsewhere, a bunch of tiny red bugs with spots descended. They were lucky ladybugs! Even grumpy Mr. Grumbles smiled at them.

But wait, there was more! Next came a collection of little beetles. They tickled everyone's feet, scurrying about without a care in the world. Caterpillars and fireflies followed, momentarily distracting the Titans from the task at hand.

"Well, this is certainly a surprise," Saba said.

"I know, right!" said Zaynab.

"Imagine all that happening while they were nesting in your hair," she continued, laughing aloud.

Saba's face went slightly pale at the thought of

that happening.

"Guys, focus!" Abdullah groaned, waving away the sparkling avalanche. "How are we ever going to find the blueprint now?"

Undeterred, Taiba grinned.

"Leave it to me!" she declared, holding out a finger. A tiny, furry snout poked out from her pocket. It was Mr. Squeaks, her super-sniffer teddy bear.

Mr. Squeaks twitched his nose excitedly and scurried off, following the faint scent. The confused Titans watched as the little bear led them on a merry chase. They followed Mr. Squeaks through a maze of junk - old tyres, a broken candy machine, and wobbly chairs. Finally, Mr. Squeaks sat down, panting like a tired puppy.

There it was! The secret blueprint.

Abdullah quickly located the file they were looking for. Opening it carefully, the Titans huddled around as Faisal began deciphering the blueprint inside.

His eyes widened as he read aloud,

"Guys, listen to this! Dr. Quirky isn't missing— he's actually planning to take over the world with his quirky inventions!"

Gasps filled the warehouse as the Titans realized the gravity of the situation.

"We have to stop him!" Taiba exclaimed, her magical teddy bears nodding in agreement.

"Whoa, look at this!" Faisal shouted, pointing at tiny writing at the bottom of the blueprint. It looked like a secret message, so tiny nobody could make it out.

Except for Mr. Smartypants, that is. Hence, the name.

They all squinted their eyes and tried to read it upside down, sideways, and even backwards.

"It says, 'Find the red thing,'" Mr. Smartypants said slowly.

"What does that mean?" Mr. Pookie Bear asked, scratching his head. It looked like he was about to cry... or pass out.

Just as Faisal opened his mouth to reply, a shadow zoomed past the window! They all jumped. Peeking through the dusty window, they caught a weird sight. A person wearing all red - a red hat, red coat, and red pants - was sneaking out the back door!

"Does anyone else see that?" Abdullah whispered, his eyes as big as saucers.

The tomato-like person hopped into a shiny red car, which tried to start but made funny 'putt-putt' sounds. The tomato person looked really annoyed and stamped their red foot. He stepped out and opened the car's bonnet.

*Perhaps evil villains can have car troubles, too.* Abdullah immediately felt better.

"We have to follow them!" Taiba yelled. They raced outside, just to find that the red car had sputtered on and was at a distance! Not far enough, though. The only problem was...

"Let's get to the car, quic-" Abdullah halted

mid-sentence, looking at his car violently hugging the nearby tree. Remembering the car crash earlier, he felt worse all over again.

Their legs felt like jelly, and their car was out of gas.

Just when they thought they were stuck, Baby Salman pointed at a shiny new car they hadn't seen until then. It had a huge red sign that said 'FREE RIDE!'

The Titans looked suspiciously at the escaping red car and the red sign on the car left behind.

"There's not much of a choice here, guys. Let's go!" Abdullah shouted. They all piled in the vehicle, their hearts pounding like crazy drums.

*Who was that red thing... or rather, the red person? And why were they in such a hurry?* The Titans had to find out!

# 7

## CHASING RED

Abdullah inspected peculiar controls. This was no ordinary car. It had blinking lights, a horn that played silly sounds, and a fuzzy, awkward steering wheel. The dashboard was a mess of buttons, levers, and flashing lights.

One button even had a tomato sticker on it.

"Alright, everyone buckle up!" Abdullah shouted, his fingers hovering over the wacky controls.

"Are you sure this thing will work?" Faisal asked, eyeing the tomato with worry.

"Only one way to find out!" Abdullah grinned, giving the lever a cautious pull.

With a turn of the key, the car roared to life—

or at least tried to. The engine coughed and then released a small, unimpressive puff of smoke. Abdullah tried pressing a big red button marked "GO," which made the car jump forward with a sudden jolt.

"Whoa!" Faisal yelped, holding onto his seat as the car veered wildly.

"Steer straight!" Taiba shouted, trying to adjust a passed-out Mr. Giggles, who had been tossed around by the car's erratic movement.

Abdullah wrestled with the steering wheel, trying to keep the car on track.

It swerved left and right, jumped over curbs, and even attempted a small, shaky spin. At one point, the windshield wipers started flapping wildly for no reason, and the horn let out a honking tune that sounded suspiciously like a duck's quack.

"Not quite what I had in mind," Faisal said with a surprised chuckle.

Taiba poked a button, and suddenly, a big red parachute deployed from the roof, causing the vehicle to slow down to a crawl.

"Oops! Wrong button!" Taiba yelped, trying to yank the parachute back in.

"We're losing tail, press on the gas, Abdullah!" Faisal warned.

Meanwhile, Mr. Smartpants and Mr. Grumbles tried to hold on as the car wobbled and veered erratically. Saba's hair was busy tugging at a gadget that was supposed to be a 'self-correcting steering wheel,' which only made the vehicle spin in circles.

"Abdullah, watch out!" Saba cried as they narrowly missed a lamppost.

"I'm trying!" Abdullah called back, wrestling with the steering wheel, which seemed to have its own ideas about where the car should go.

"Whoa! What does this button do?" Taiba asked, pointing to one that had a picture of a red heart.

"Let's find out!" Mr. Fluffykins said, pressing the button. The vehicle's 'Turbo Boost' kicked in unexpectedly, and they zoomed down the street, narrowly missing a burger stand. The vendor, covered in mustard, waved his fist angrily.

But the Titans were too focused on their chase to notice.

"Keep an eye out for the red figure!" Abdullah shouted.

"And don't touch anyth-!"

Zaynab, wanting to help, pressed the red SOS button. This activated the bubble blaster mode, sending a barrage of bubbles out the back.

"Oops! I didn't mean to press that!" she exclaimed, trying to shut it off.

The bubbles surrounded them, making it hard to see. In the midst of the chaos, Faisal spotted a flash of red darting down an alley.

"There! Follow that red thing!"

Abdullah swerved, making the vehicle spin in a dizzying circle before it straightened out and raced into the alley. They were closing in on the figure when the car suddenly lurched to the side.

"What now?" Saba asked as her hair bobbed around in the turbulence.

Abdullah gritted his teeth and tried to maintain control as the car's suspension bounced them around like a bouncy castle.

"Hang on!" Abdullah shouted, making a sharp turn.

"Uh, it looks like the 'Hover Mode' is malfunctioning!"

The car hovered awkwardly, tipping from side to side.

"Hold on!" Faisal called out as they swung around another corner.

A loud bang came from the rear, and the car's exhaust pipe shot out a puff of smoke that made the windows foggy. The headlights flickered on and off, and one of the tyres started making a strange squeaky noise.

Abdullah was barely able to keep his balance as the vehicle swerved and spun. Through the confusion and chaos, they caught sight of the red figure... his tall, awkward stature and exaggerated movements made him stand out like a sore thumb.

"There he is!" Faisal shouted, pointing excitedly.

The red figure, now out of the car and clearly visible, was running towards a towering brick building. The Titans quickly realized that the red figure was not the most graceful individual. He stumbled over his own feet, his red coat flapping comically. As he dashed down the road, his red hat bobbed up and down, nearly falling off every few seconds.

The Titans' vehicle finally landed back on the ground with a *thud*, and Abdullah slammed the accelerator. They zoomed past the building, and Abdullah slammed on the brakes.

"Out! Out! We need to catch him on foot!" Abdullah yelled.

The Titans scrambled out of the vehicle and sprinted towards the building.

The red figure glanced back, their eyes widening with surprise as the car skidded in their direction. The figure picked up the pace, dodging between pedestrians and parked cars, almost at the door. They could see his red hat and coat flapping wildly as he ran.

As the Titans reached the door, it slammed shut just as they got close. Taiba tried to open it, but it was locked tight.

"It's locked! What do we do now?" she asked.

Faisal examined the door.

"There's got to be another way in. Maybe around the side?"

The Titans dashed around the side of the building and found a window slightly ajar. Faisal used his flashlight to peer inside.

"I think we can squeeze through here!"

One by one, they wriggled through the window and landed inside. The room was dimly lit, filled with strange gadgets and mysterious blueprints scattered across a table.

"There he is!" Saba whispered urgently, spotting the red figure pacing nervously in the corner. He was holding a stack of papers.

The red figure looked up at them with wide eyes.

"Whoa! You caught me!" he said, trying to straighten his hat and coat, which were now askew.

"Why were you running?" Faisal demanded. "Do you know something about Dr. Quirky?"

The red figure gulped, his face turning as red as his outfit.

"Well, I do know a thing or two. He's hiding in a secure building on the city's outskirts. The Oracle."

The Titans looked at each other in shock.

"The Oracle?" Taiba asked.

"Yes," the red figure nodded vigorously.

"It's heavily guarded, but that's where you'll find Dr. Quirky. I was supposed to keep you away, but... well, you're obviously quite persistent."

"And brave," Zaynab added with a smile.

The red figure's eyes twinkled with a hint of relief.

"Yes, exactly. So, if you're looking for Dr. Quirky..." The red figure hesitated, then sighed.

"Alright, I'll tell you. But first, you need to know—"

Suddenly, the building began to rumble, and the lights flickered. The Titans looked at each other in alarm.

"What's happening?" Abdullah asked.

The red figure's eyes widened in fear.

"It's a trap! Dr. Quirky must have set this up!"

The room shook again, and the walls started closing in, making the situation even more urgent.

"What do we do now?" Zaynab asked, her powerful voice trembling slightly.

The red figure clutched the papers tightly.

"You need to get out of here quickly! I'll help you, but we need to move fast!"

With that, the red figure dashed towards a hidden door in the back of the room. The Titans followed, their hearts pounding as the walls continued to close in.

The door creaked open, revealing a narrow escape tunnel.

"This way!" the red figure shouted.

The Titans rushed through the tunnel, and just as they reached the end, the tunnel collapsed behind them. They tumbled out into the open air, gasping for breath.

They looked back at the building, which was now silent and still.

"That was too close!" Taiba said, trying to calm her racing heart.

The red figure turned to them, his expression serious.

"Dr. Quirky is planning something big. You need to find out what's in this blueprint and notes I managed to save."

He handed the stack of papers to Faisal.

"Good luck. And be careful. Dr. Quirky won't stop until he's taken over everything."

The Titans nodded. With that, he gave them a shaky salute and hurried away, his red coat flapping behind him. They glanced at the papers, their curiosity piqued. What secrets did they hold?

The Titans returned to their unpredictable car, which was now making a funny gurgling noise. Abdullah gave a sheepish grin as he turned the key. The car sputtered to life once again, albeit reluctantly. But with every jolt and hiccup of the car, one thing was clear: the adventure was far from finished, and they had to uncover the mysteries and stop Dr. Quirky before it was too late.

The Titans exchanged glances. The Oracle was the next place they needed to go.

# 8

## LOUD AND CLEAR

The Titans huddled together, staring at the massive building before them. The Oracle, this was it. According to the tip from the red man, this was where Dr. Quirky was hiding.

"This place looks like a secret spy base!" Abdullah said, staring at the tall fence with barbed wire and sparks flying off it.

"And it's locked up tighter than Mum locks candy jars!" Taiba added, pointing at the huge padlock on the gate. The padlock had a silly face painted on it, with big, wiggly eyes that seemed to watch them.

Zaynab grinned, stepping forward with a confidence that only she could muster in such a weird situation.

"I've got this!" she declared, flexing her fingers as if warming up for a vocal performance.

The others quickly covered their ears. They knew what was coming. Zaynab took a deep breath, puffing up her cheeks, and then let out her famous screech. The sound shot towards the gate, smashing the padlock into tiny pieces.

But Zaynab's screech did more than just break the lock. The noise was so loud that car alarms started blaring in the parking lot. Lights flashed, and a nearby mailbox started spitting out letters. Even a flock of pigeons took off, squawking in surprise.

"Oops!" Zaynab giggled, covering her mouth.

"Well, that worked!" Faisal struggled to suppress his laughter.

"Let's get inside before the whole neighbourhood comes running!"

They pushed the gate open and ran to the building's entrance. There, a big steel door stood, looking very tough. Next to it was an intercom with a funny little speaker.

"Welcome! Please state your purpose or prepare for tickle lasers!" a minion voice chirped, followed by a series of creepy giggles.

"Tickle lasers?!" Taiba exclaimed, half-amused and half-confused.

"Round two, Zaynab?" Abdullah suggested.

"My pleasure, stand back!" Zaynab said, taking another deep breath. She unleashed another ear-splitting screech. The door trembled as if laughing at a bad joke before the lock gave up and burst open with a loud pop.

Inside, the building was filled with strange gadgets. There were conveyor belts with rubber chickens, toilet paper hanging from the ceiling, and walls lined with what looked like parts from old vacuum cleaners. Each gadget had a silly name like 'Dustinator 3000' and 'Lint Launcher.'

"This place is so weird!" Abdullah whispered as a mechanical arm waved at them.

"Stay close, everyone," Faisal said, trying to sound brave.

"We need to find Dr. Quirky."

They sneaked through the hallways, trying not

to make a sound. One room was filled with mannequins dressed like superheroes, and another had a giant hamster wheel with a cardboard cutout of Dr. Quirky looking very pleased with himself.

After a while, they found a door that was slightly open. Abdullah pushed it carefully, and they peeked inside. The room was packed with even more strange gadgets and a big control panel covered with buttons and lights.

In the corner, they spotted a rug with a lump underneath. They pulled it back and found an escape route guarded by a small robotic duck. The duck had a shiny helmet and wheels, and it quacked at them like it was guarding something of great importance.

"A hidden passage!" Abdullah whispered, pointing at it.

Taiba eyed the robotic duck. The duck seemed to be eyeing them back as if daring them to make a move.

"We have to find Dr. Quirky," Faisal said firmly.

"I'll handle the duck." He grabbed a nearby stuffed cat and tossed it toward the robot. The duck instantly chased after it, quacking furiously as it tried to wrestle the stuffed animal.

With the coast clear, they pulled open the exit door and found a narrow staircase leading down. The stairs were lined with neon lights, giving off a weird glow.

"I hope there aren't any spiders," Saba whispered as they descended.

The air got colder and smelled funny, like a mix of candy and old socks. They reached the bottom and entered a big underground room. The walls were covered in glowing tubes filled with bubbling goo. In the middle of the room stood a bizarre contraption that looked like a cross between a medieval siege engine and a giant cat tree. It was covered in plush scratching posts, dangling toys, and rotating laser pointers, all connected to a complex network of gears and levers.

"What is that thing?" Faisal asked, scratching his head.

"It looks like... a giant cat playground?" Taiba guessed.

"Maybe it's controlling all the gadgets and security stuff in the building," Abdullah said, though he wasn't entirely convinced.

Just then, they heard a noise. They turned to see a figure stepping out of the shadows. It was Dr. Quirky in the flesh. He wore a suit and tie that looked like it came straight out of a thrift store from the 1970s, and over it, he sported an apron with a goofy slogan: 'Pawsitively the Best Scientist!'

He had a head full of wild, curly hair that seemed to be in a constant state of rebellion, and his hairline was on an epic journey of retreat. His smile was so wide it looked like it might just wrap around his head, but it was about as warm as a freezer full of ice cream. Even Zaynab felt a shiver go down her spine.

"Well, well, well," Dr. Quirky said in a sing-song

manner,

"You've made it this far, but can you handle the Feline Frenzy 9000?" He struck a pose next to the ridiculous machine, which now whirred and clattered with an array of silly cat sounds and flashing lights.

"One wrong move and you might unleash a cat-tastrophe!"

The Titans looked at each other, trying not to laugh. The whole scene was so absurdly childish, but they knew they had to stop Dr. Quirky's crazy plans.

When Dr. Quirky noticed the Titans eyeing his apron with curiosity, he quickly unbuttoned it and slipped it off, trying to hide the overly affectionate slogan while awkwardly balancing it behind his back.

"Get ready, Titans," Abdullah said, trying to keep a straight face.

"This is going to be... interesting."

"You won't get away with your evil plans, Dr. Quirky!" Saba shouted.

"Oh, but I already have," Dr. Quirky sneered.

"You see, you're too late. My plan is already in action, and soon, I'll have complete control over everything!"

Abdullah quickly approached the control panel and started pressing buttons, trying to figure out the cat machine.

Dr. Quirky's eyes widened in panic as he rushed toward Abdullah.

"What are you doing?!" he shouted.

Before Dr. Quirky could reach him, Faisal stepped into his path. But instead of blocking him physically, he began talking.

"Ah, Dr. Quirky! Allow me to elucidate the intricacies of the situation with some perspicuous perspicacity and a bit of linguistic legerdemain! Forsooth, if thou wouldst indulge in a cacophony of convoluted circumlocutions and a diaphanous diatribe of dexterous diction, thou might find thine comprehension utterly befuddled!"

Dr. Quirky halted, utterly confused. His eyes

glazed over as he tried to follow Faisal's direction of speech. "What... are you even saying? What on earth does that even—?"

In the chaos, Abdullah's fingers flew over the buttons of the Feline Frenzy 9000. The machine whirred and buzzed with increasing intensity, the lights flashing erratically. Abdullah spotted the big red switch labelled 'Emergency Shutdown' and pounced on it.

"This has to be it," Abdullah muttered to himself, yanking the switch with all his might.

"It means *you lose*," Faisal replied the scientist, pointing at Abdullah.

The machine emitted a loud, screeching noise before going completely silent. The lights stopped flashing, and the whirring noise faded away. The once chaotic contraption now stood still, its whimsical cat sounds silenced.

"You did it!" Taiba cheered.

Dr. Quirky, his confusion now turning to

frustration, let out a high-pitched, dramatic scream.

"No! This isn't over yet!" He turned and sprinted toward a hidden door at the back of the chamber.

"After him!" Faisal shouted, urging the team into action.

The Titans sprinted after Dr. Quirky. But just as they were about to catch up to him, he disappeared through the door, slamming it shut behind him.

They tried to open the door, but it was locked tight.

"He's getting away!" Zaynab cried, pounding on the door in frustration.

"Wait, look!" Taiba said, pointing to a small panel next to the door. It was another control panel with a keypad.

"If we can figure out the code, we can open the door," Abdullah said, examining the keypad.

The team tried a few obvious combinations: the scientist's birthday and then his mum's, and even his favourite cat Twinkle Toes's... Faisal apparently did his research. Still, each attempt was met with a loud buzz and a flashing red light.

"This is harder than we thought!" Faisal said, pacing back and forth.

"What could Dr. Quirky use as a code?"

Zaynab's eyes sparkled with an idea.

"Wait, remember when Dr. Quirky bragged about how clever and unpredictable he was? He mentioned something about creating a password that was completely impossible to guess."

"Really?" Abdullah asked, intrigued.

"What did he say?"

"He made a big deal about having the most unguessable code ever. He even joked that it was 'so secret, even his cats couldn't guess it!'" Zaynab explained with a grin.

"Hmm," Faisal said, scratching his chin thoughtfully.

"If he was that confident, it's probably

something ridiculously obvious but designed to throw us off."

Abdullah nodded, his fingers poised over the keypad.

"Alright, let's try something completely out of left field. How about we go with... '0000'?"

The team exchanged amused looks as Abdullah typed in the password.

The keypad beeped once, twice, then let out a triumphant ding sound, and the door swung open with a theatrical whoosh.

They were ready to catch Dr. Quirky. But instead of finding another hallway, they stumbled into a small, dimly lit room with nothing but a single lightbulb hanging from the ceiling and a few dusty old boxes.

"Where did he go?" Taiba asked, looking around with wide eyes.

"He must have another way out," Abdullah said, his voice echoing in the empty room as he searched the walls for secret passages.

As they investigated, Faisal noticed something odd—a loose panel on the floor that looked out of place.

"Hey, look at this!" he said, kneeling down and prying it open. Beneath it was a trapdoor with a large, cartoonish handle.

"Down here!" Faisal called out, excitedly pointing at it.

They all grabbed the handle and pulled with a united effort. The door creaked open, revealing a dark staircase leading further underground. They descended the stairs, their hearts pounding wild in their chests.

At the bottom, they found themselves in another underground chamber, this one even larger and more cluttered than the last. The walls were covered in strange gadgets, blueprints, and all sorts of bizarre contraptions. In the centre of the room stood an enormous control panel covered in blinking lights and twisting knobs.

"You guessed it!" Dr. Quirky said, clapping his hands with exaggerated enthusiasm.

"You actually figured out my password! I thought it was foolproof!"

The Titans couldn't help but smirk at the sight of Dr. Quirky's over-the-top celebration and the sheer absurdity of the room.

"Guess you weren't as sneaky as you thought!" Faisal said.

Dr. Quirky looked momentarily deflated but quickly recovered with a dramatic sigh.

"Well, you may have cracked the code, but you'll still have to get through my ultimate trap! Welcome to my lair, Titans. This is where the real action happens."

That said, the Titans braced themselves for the next part of their quirky quest.

# 9

## SLIME TIME

**D**r. Quirky suddenly dashed off. Off across the lair and yanked open a door labelled

'Fire Exit.'

The Titans pursued him as he charged up the stairs. Faisal led the way, holding a flashlight, with Abdullah and Zaynab close behind. Taiba and her army of teddies struggled to catch up, along with Saba, who carried Baby Salman. The little guy quietly sucked on his thumb, enjoying the human rollercoaster.

They all huffed and puffed as they climbed, their legs hurting now.

Finally, they reached a wider hallway, and with a few more steps, the staircase led them to the rooftop. Dr. Quirky, already halfway up a shiny helicopter, was giving them an enthusiastic salute. The helicopter's blades whirred as it lifted off into the sky.

"Ughh!" Faisal groaned, hands on his knees. "We were so close!"

"No, we weren't," Mr. Smartypants said truthfully.

Before Faisal could come up with a reply, Mr. Squeaks let out a series of squeaks, calling them over to him. When the Titans reached Mr. Squeaks, they found a bright red furry box with the words 'Open Me with a Smile' written on it.

The Titans didn't even try. In fact, their facial muscles strained down, down into a frown. Faisal grabbed the box and immediately started tearing it apart.

Inside, they found a heart-shaped note with a riddle:

*"Down you must go to where things get quite serious,*
*Find the control panel, and act not delirious.*
*Ask a wise person when your quest seems unclear,*
*For guidance from someone who's dear."*

The Titans exchanged puzzled glances.

"Hmm, that sounds like we need to head back downstairs and check out the control panel," Abdullah said.

Reluctantly, they descended the stairs, realizing just how clever Dr. Quirky was.

It was clear now—this was all part of his plan. He was more than just quirky; he was a mastermind, maybe even smarter than Faisal, which Faisal found hard to admit.

The scenery had changed. The lair's slick and shiny floor welcomed them. The eerie glow from the tubes made everything look like it was bathed in green slime.

"Careful, everyone," Abdullah warned.

"The floor looks super slippery."

Just as he finished speaking, there was a faint clatter. Out of nowhere emerged a peculiar figure—a small, scrappy robot cat with one red and one blue eye. Its tail stood up like a wild tuft of hair, and it clutched a tiny metallic device. The cat robot had a mischievous grin that could only mean trouble.

"Stop right there!" Faisal shouted, trying to sound brave.

The cat robot smirked, clearly not impressed. But as it took a step back, its foot slipped on the slick floor. It wobbled, flailed its arms, and then crashed down with a loud *thud*.

Baby Salman, startled by the commotion, let out a tiny whimper.

Suddenly, a large drop of drool fell from Baby Salman's mouth and slid right next to the cat-robot-thing. The drool began to pool and spread, making the floor even more slippery. The villain, now struggling to get up, slipped and slid in every direction.

Taiba couldn't help but laugh,

"Looks like Baby Salman's got him trapped!"

The thing tried to get to its feet, but its legs splayed out, causing him to fall again. He dropped the device he was holding, which skidded across the floor and stopped at Faisal's feet. Faisal picked it up, eyes wide with curiosity.

"What's this?" Faisal wondered aloud.

"Give that back! It's mine!" it shouted, still

struggling.

"Finders keepers!" Faisal retorted, holding the device up like a trophy.

The cat managed to sit up, looking more embarrassed than menacing.

"You think this is funny? You'll be sorry!"

"Oh, we're already sorry," Taiba giggled.

"Sorry that you're so bad at staying on your feet!"

The villain cat, trying to regain some dignity, stood up shakily. But just as it did, Baby Salman let out a happy gurgle, and another stream of drool flowed onto the floor.

The villain's eyes widened in horror as he slipped again, landing flat on his back with a loud *splat*.

The scene was too ridiculous not to enjoy. The cat looked like a fish out of water, flapping and flopping in the puddle of drool. Even Mr. Giggles, who had been quiet the whole time, let out a chuckle.

"Okay, okay, let's focus," Abdullah said, trying

to regain composure.

He looked at the device in Faisal's hand. It was a small, boxy gadget with a screen and a few buttons.

"This thing might be important. Let's see what it does."

As they examined the device, the villain finally managed to get to his feet, using the wall for support. He glared at them, clearly upset, but he didn't dare move towards the drool-covered floor again.

"What does it do?" Zaynab asked, peering over Faisal's shoulder.

Faisal pressed a button, and the screen lit up. A series of numbers and letters flashed across the display. He frowned, trying to make sense of it.

"It looks like some kind of code," he said.

"But I don't know what it means."

The android cat smirked despite its predicament.

"You'll never figure it out," he sneered.

"That's the key to Dr. Quirky's master plan!

You'll never stop him!"

The Titans exchanged glances.

The stakes were getting higher. This little device held vital information that could help them stop Dr. Quirky. They had to find a way to decode it.

"Looks like we've got our next mission," Abdullah said. He pocketed the device, giving the villain a final look.

"Thanks for the tip."

With that, they turned and headed back up the stairs, leaving the disgruntled cat robot to deal with the mess they'd left behind. The Titans couldn't help but laugh as they replayed the scene in their minds. Baby Salman, oblivious to his heroics, cooed contentedly.

Just as they were about to pile into the strange car again, Abdullah pulled out the heart-shaped riddle from his pocket and stared at it.

"I think we need to talk to Grandpa!"

Everyone turned to him, puzzled.

"I know you miss riding your bicycle with him, Abdullah," Faisal said with concern.

"But there's a mission to finish first."

"No, I mean, he's so wise," Abdullah clarified.

"Yeah, Grandpa did get good marks in physics," Taiba said, scratching her head. "And that's saying something! But what does that have to do with anything?"

"I think he hurt his head," Mr. Pookie Bear gossiped from behind.

"Maybe it's the slip he had when we were chasing Dr. Wacky Wacky." Mr. Fluffykins quipped, impersonating the whole scene.

"I think he's finally realizing he doesn't know how to drive," Mr. Grumbles grumbled.

"I know how to drive!" Abdullah shot back,

"In fact, I can—"

"Guys, relax," Taiba ordered her teddy bears.

"Let Abdullah explain."

As everyone settled down, Abdullah continued,

"Who's the wisest person we know and hold dear... if not Grandpa?" Then he showed them the heart-shaped paper.

A lightbulb seemed to go off in everyone's heads, and they gasped in agreement.

"Let's get back to Grandpa and figure this out," Faisal said, holding up the device.

"We're one step closer to stopping Dr. Quirky!"

The group cheered, and off they went to meet their wise grandad.

# 10

## THE WISE GRANDAD

The Titans laughed all the way to their grandad's, thinking about the rooftop escapade. As they drove, Faisal couldn't help but glance at the device in his hand.

The device was a quirky little gadget, much like something Dr. Quirky himself would invent. It was boxy, with bright, winking buttons. A tiny antenna bobbed up and down, and a picture of a cheerful, animated face sat in the middle of the screen. It looked more like a toy than a high-tech device, but Faisal knew it held something important. The anticipation of the unknown made the drive feel longer than usual.

When they finally arrived, they were greeted

by the cosy smell of old books and freshly baked cookies. Their grandad's house was warm and inviting, with shelves full of knick-knacks and a soft, comfy couch in the living room. Grandad himself, a tall man with a white beard and twinkling eyes, stood there adjusting his old-fashioned suit and pocket watch.

"Grandpa!" they shouted in unison, rushing to him.

"Ah, my little troublesolvers," Grandad said with a warm smile.

"What brings you here in such a hurry?"

Abdullah quickly explained their encounter with Dr. Quirky and the mysterious device they had found. He handed the device to Grandad, who inspected it thoughtfully.

He turned it over in his hands.

"Hmm, quite the peculiar gadget," Grandad murmured, stroking his beard.

"It seems to hold some secrets."

The children watched eagerly as Grandad took

a seat in his favourite armchair, the one with the big cushions that always seemed to swallow him up. He leaned back, and they gathered around him, sitting cross-legged on the floor.

"Now, let's see," Grandad began, his voice calm and soothing.

"The riddle you found said you must go where things get serious. That's an interesting clue."

Faisal nodded, holding up the heart-shaped note.

"Yeah, and it also said to ask a wise person when our quest seems unclear."

"Well, you've come to the right place!" Grandad chuckled.

"Let's think about this together."

He paused, staring into space as if deep in thought. The children fidgeted, excited and impatient. Saba couldn't hold back her curiosity.

"Grandpa, are you gonna tell us where to go?" she blurted out.

Grandad chuckled again.

"Patience, my dear. Wisdom isn't always about knowing the answers right away. Sometimes, it's about asking the right questions."

The kids looked at each other, puzzled. Abdullah raised his hand.

"Okay, then, what questions should we ask?"

"Good question!" Grandad said, nodding approvingly.

"Let's start with what we know. This device," he held it up. "It has numbers and letters, correct?"

Faisal nodded.

"Yeah, but we can't figure out what they mean."

Grandad leaned forward and poked one of the buttons. The screen lit up, and the animated face spoke in a squeaky, high-pitched voice.

"Hello, Grandpa. Hello, Titans! I'm Gizmo, your guide to chaos and mayhem!"

Taiba giggled.

"Is this thing serious?"

Gizmo's eyes on the screen rolled playfully.

"Absolutely! I'm here to help you, but only if you can keep up with my wacky riddles and challenges! Ready, set, go!"

The screen changed, showing a cartoon map with a big, red X marked on it. Gizmo grinned and said,

"Dr. Quirky's next target is... somewhere you'll never guess! Hint: It's a place where things go round and round!"

The Titans gave an exasperated look.

"I don't think Gizmo's updated with the latest version," Zaynab said with one eyebrow raised.

"We're past the merry-go-round level."

Grandpa gave the gadget a hard tap and slam,

"Maybe that'll fix it."

Gizmo beeped and booed.

"Ouch Grandpa!... No wonder there is less tech and more books here. We don't do that anymore." Said Abdullah.

The gadget gave a deep sigh.

Grandpa held his hands up in surrender. Satisfied, it turned to the Titans.

"Wait," Faisal said, thinking hard.

"What about a roundabout? You know, those spinning rides in playgrounds?"

Gizmo nodded enthusiastically.

"Ding ding! You're getting closer! But there's more to it. You'll need to use your brains and brawn to figure out the exact spot!"

The Titans leaned in, trying to decipher the map. Gizmo continued to giggle and make funny faces, keeping them on their toes.

Abdullah pointed to a spot on the map.

"What about the big Ferris wheel in the abandoned park? It still goes round in circles!"

Gizmo's face lit up with a big grin.

"Bingo! But beware! Dr. Quirky's planning something wild and wacky there. He's got gadgets and many evil gizmos ready to cause chaos!"

The children gasped. This was serious, but this quirky Gizmo's playful nature made it all seem like a big, fun game. They loved the idea of stopping Dr. Quirky's latest plan, though.

"Okay, Gizmo, tell us more!" Faisal urged, eager to learn how to stop Dr. Quirky.

Gizmo waggled its antenna.

"Nope! That's all for now! If you want to know more, you'll have to play my game! But hurry, the clock is ticking!"

The screen showed a ticking countdown, adding to the urgency. The Titans knew they had to act fast. With Gizmo as their ally, they were ready to head to the park and figure out what Dr. Quirky was up to.

"Good luck, Titans! Remember, have fun and keep smiling! Even if you get dizzy!" With that, Gizmo shut down, its battery percentage at zero.

So much for being an ally...

Faisal looked at the now blank device.

"So, we need to go to the abandoned park?"

Grandad nodded.

"It seems that way. But remember, whatever you find, approach it with wisdom and courage." He stared at each of his grandchildren,

"Sometimes, things might seem confusing or scary, but if you stay positive and work together, you can overcome any challenge."

The kids nodded, feeling inspired. Abdullah hugged Grandad, beaming with joy.

"Thanks, Grandpa. You always know what to say."

Grandad chuckled, patting Abdullah's head.

"Just remember, I'm always here if you need more wisdom or just a good old-fashioned hug."

Their spirits were lifted now, and the Titans knew what they had to do. They thanked their grandad, promising to be careful and smart. As they headed out the door, Grandad called after them,

"And don't forget to smile! Even in danger, a smile can be your greatest weapon!"

The children laughed and waved goodbye. They had a new mission, a riddle to solve, and the wisdom of their grandad to guide them. With pockets full of determination, they were more than ready for the next chapter of their adventure.

# 11

## THE HEART OF THE MATTER

The Titans gathered in their crimson car and shot off toward Central London. As they approached the park, an eerie silence fell over them.

The kids climbed out of the car and stood still

momentarily, taking in the spooky scene.

The abandoned park was composed of rusty playground equipment that creaked in the breeze. Wild bushes swayed gently, and in the distance, the Ferris wheel circled around slowly, its creaky metal groaning like a tired giant. The signboard had also fallen off the hinges —the signboard that said 'Puddleton Park.'

Faisal squinted up at the Ferris wheel, which seemed to watch them back with its enormous, spinning eye.

"This place gives me the creeps," Zaynab whispered, hugging herself.

"That makes all of us," Mr. Smartypants replied.

"Let's get this over with," Faisal said, trying to sound brave for his siblings and their bears.

"Gizmo says Dr. Quirky's plan involves the Ferris wheel. We have to stop him!"

Just then, Gizmo sprang to life with a childish

giggle.

"Remember, the answer lies in finding the heart of the matter!" Gizmo's screen flickered with a bright, heart-shaped symbol before fading to normal.

"Another riddle," Abdullah murmured, shaking his head.

"Let's all pan out and search for clues."

The kids spread out, searching for anything suspicious. Taiba's teddy bears waddled around like tiny detectives on a mission. Mr. Sqeaky's nose twitched as he sniffed the air, his button eyes narrowing with speculation.

Suddenly, Mr. Squeaky froze, his fuzzy paw raised. He pointed towards a bush that looked particularly overgrown, its branches thick and tangled.

"I think Mr. Squeaky found something!" Taiba whispered excitedly.

They all gathered around the bush, peering into the shadows. The leaves rustled softly. Faisal stepped closer and carefully pushed the branches aside. Hidden beneath the thick foliage was a small, heart-shaped door covered in vines, almost like it had been waiting for them to find it.

"Wow!" Zaynab gasped. "It's just like the riddle said!"

Abdullah knelt down and examined the door. "This must be it. The heart of the matter."

Faisal reached out and turned the handle. The door creaked open, revealing a dark, narrow tunnel that led deep underground. The air inside was cool and damp, carrying the smell of earth and mystery.

"Great job, teddy bears!" Taiba said, patting Mr. Squeaky.

"Let's see where this goes."

"Let's go," Faisal said, his voice echoing slightly in the tunnel.

The kids hesitated momentarily, then stepped inside, one by one. Taiba scooped up her teddy bears and held them close as they entered the darkness. Gizmo floated beside them, its light casting long shadows on the tunnel walls.

As they walked, the tunnel twisted and turned, and the only sound was the soft scuffling of their shoes on the dirt floor. Suddenly, Mr. Fluffykins, not paying attention, waddled right into a thin wire stretched across the path.

*SNAP!*

A loud clanking sound reverberated through the tunnel as the wire triggered a trap.

"Oh no!" Zaynab gasped.

"What did he do?"

The walls began to close in, threatening to squish them.

"Run!" Abdullah shouted.

The kids scrambled to find a way out. Gizmo beeped frantically,

"Press the red button on my side! Hurry!"

Faisal fumbled with Gizmo and finally managed to press the button just in time. The walls stopped moving, leaving the kids squished together, laughing nervously.

"Nice going, Mr. Fluffykins," Taiba said, wiping sweat from her forehead.

"Maybe next time, watch where you're going."

Mr. Fluffykins just blinked his button eyes, looking innocent.

They continued down the tunnel, now more cautious of traps. With every few steps, Gizmo would beep a warning sound, helping them tiptoe around pressure plates or duck under tripwires. But the teddy bears, despite their best efforts, kept accidentally setting off the traps, turning the serious mission into a comedy.

Once, Mr. Grumbles accidentally stepped on a dart trap, causing darts to shoot from the walls. Luckily, they all ducked just in time, and one dart harmlessly bounced off Mr. Grumbles' plush belly, making him tumble backwards with a soft thud.

The kids couldn't help but giggle, even as they dodged the traps. The teddy bears' clumsy antics made it all the more ridiculous.

After what felt like hours, they reached the end of the tunnel and found themselves in a large underground chamber. The room had blinking lights, strange gadgets, and whirring machines. It looked like a mad scientist's workshop, with calculations scribbled across the tables and wires hanging from the ceiling.

"Yet another Quirky lab... out of all the unexpected places... what is this evil villain up to," Abdullah muttered.

Gizmo hovered over to a massive control panel in the centre of the room.

"Careful, Titans. This place is full of dangerous devices."

It was the first time the Titans had heard Gizmo talk in all his seriousness. That's when they knew things were getting serious.

And so, they were—as careful as the Titans could very well be.

The kids tiptoed around, examining the strange

contraptions. They found a machine that looked like it could shoot popcorn, a helmet with wires sticking out in all directions, self-washing socks, and even a pair of boots with springs on the bottom. It was like walking through a crazy inventor's dream, which explained Dr. Quirky's essence to the T.

Now, they were a clumsy lot, so naturally, things didn't quite go as planned.

As they explored, Mr. Fluffykins sashayed over to the control panel and pressed a big red button before anyone could stop him. A hidden door slid open with a loud *whoosh*, revealing a room filled with even more gadgets. But these were different—sharper, more meaner-looking.

The air buzzed with tension as they realized they had stumbled upon something much more dangerous than they had anticipated. The kids exchanged nervous glances, knowing they had to be careful.

"We need to figure out what these are and stop

Dr. Quirky," Faisal said.

Before they could investigate further, a loud alarm blared. Red lights flashed, and the ground shook.

"Uh-oh," Saba said.

"I think we triggered the security system." She eyed Baby Salman, who was busy playing peek-a-boo with the alarm system.

The room filled with the sounds of whirring machines and clanking gears. The teddy bears clung to Taiba, their button eyes wide with fear and excitement. The Titans braced themselves as the lab seemed to come to life around them.

# 12

## THE SHOWDOWN

Saba took a deep breath, trying to calm her racing heart.

"Alright, everyone, let's be careful. We don't know what these things can do."

Looking around, they noticed gadgets lined up against the walls, each one stranger than the last.

On a sleek counter sat the Sassy Speaker, its tiny speaker glaring with passive-aggressive fury. Nearby, the Chatterbox Speaker hummed to itself, waiting to interrupt anyone who dared to speak.

The Moody Thermostat flickered its temperature display, its mood clearly set to "**bad**." Its screen flashed different temperatures like it couldn't make up its mind. One minute, it was freezing cold, making everyone shiver, and the next, it was boiling hot, making them sweat. The air seemed to change with its every mood swing.

Hovering above them was the Drone of Miscommunication, buzzing around like an angry bee, just waiting to send the wrong message to the wrong person. Ironically, the small flying machine seemed to laugh at them as it flew by. It kept sending out confusing messages, mixing up their names, and causing all kinds of misunderstandings.

Before they could plan their next move, the gadgets sprang to life. The lab buzzed with energy as each device prepared to defend its territory.

The Mean Vacuum attacked first, a round robot that zoomed around with a loud buzzing noise. It had sharp bristles spinning underneath, and it seemed to know exactly where to find the dustiest spots. But as it cleaned, it shot out tiny puffs of dust, making the Titans cough and rub their eyes. The vacuum had its eyes on the teddy bears, ready to pounce like a cat stalking a mouse.

The teddy bears scrambled in all directions, their tiny feet skidding on the slick floor. Mr. Pookie Bear tried to charge at the Mean Vacuum but slipped and landed on his fluffy bottom. In this interim, Mr. Fluffykins got tangled in the vacuum's cord, spinning around like a top. Just when it looked like the bears were doomed, they accidentally knocked over a shelf of dust bunnies. The vacuum, overwhelmed, choked and sputtered before shutting down.

The bears high-fived each other, victorious but wobbling on their feet.

And there, sitting on a shelf, was the Annoying Alarm Clock. Its red numbers flashed 07:00 A.M. over and over again, taunting them with the threat of an ear-splitting ring. Zaynab eyed it warily, knowing that at any moment, it would unleash its piercing sound.

Sure enough, it let out an ear-piercing ring that made everyone jump. But Zaynab wasn't one to be outdone. She took a deep breath and let out her own screech, matching the clock's tone. The two screeched at each other, back and forth, until the clock's display started flickering, unable to keep up with Zaynab's powerful lungs.

In the corner, Saba caught sight of the Rude Mirror, a tall, shiny object with a smooth, reflective surface. As Saba approached, the mirror's surface rippled like water, and then it showed her a messy version of her reflection.

"Ugh, seriously?" it sneered, its voice dripping with sarcasm.

"You call that a hairstyle? That ponytail is so

last year,"

"Oh yeah?" Saba smirked.

"Let's see what my hair thinks!" Sensing the insult, they bristled with energy.

"Oh, it's on!" Saba grinned, letting her hair loose. It shot out like living tendrils, wrapping around the mirror's frame, tugging and pulling as if trying to give it a makeover of its own. The mirror, taken aback, attempted to reflect a dozen different styles at once, but Saba's hair was too quick, tangling it up in knots.

Meanwhile, Abdullah was eyeing the Twisty Spinner—a quirky robot with big, googly eyes and helicopter propellers for arms. The Twisty Spinner spun around in circles, shooting out ribbons that wrapped around everything in sight.

"You think a few ribbons are gonna stop me?" Abdullah grinned, gripping the wheel.

But the ribbons were stretchy, and the Twisty Whirler tugged back as he pulled. Abdullah grabbed the steering wheel of a nearby cart, but the ribbons tangled around it, making the wheel spin wildly.

"Not today!" Abdullah shouted, tugging back as the Twisty Spinner tried to take control.

Baby Salman was giggling at the Tickle Ball, a round, bouncy robot with tiny feathers sticking out on the other side of the lab. The ball-shaped robot's feather-like appendages wiggled playfully, tickling Baby Salman's cheeks and sides. His giggles turned into a full-on belly laugh, and soon, drool started to drip down his chin.

The more he laughed, the more drool there was, turning the floor into a slippery mess. The evil machine slipped one time and another, then another, as Baby Salman observed it with wide eyes.

On a table close by, the Sassy Speaker sat with its screen glowing a soft blue. Its screen displaying a sarcastic smiley face. Every few seconds, it emitted a soft chime, like it was mocking them, daring them to give it a command. Faisal could already feel the headache forming as he prepared to engage with it.

The Chatterbox Speaker blinked hypnotically next to it. It was a tall, cylindrical device with lights that blinked in a circle.

Faisal squared off with the Sassy Speaker first. "Turn off!" he commanded, his voice firm.

"Did you mean 'turn on'?" the speaker replied in a sing-song voice, clearly trying to be difficult.

"No, turn OFF!" Faisal repeated, feeling his patience wear thin.

"Playing your least favourite sounds now!" the speaker chirped, blasting a high-pitched whine that made Faisal cover his ears. The speaker seemed to delight in twisting his words.

At the same time, the Chatterbox Speaker intervened in the verbal fight. Every time Faisal tried to speak, it interrupted him with some random advice.

"You should really consider being quieter," it interrupted.

"I think we should sort this out—" Faisal started.

"According to my calculations, you should do nothing!" the speaker blared, cutting him off.

"But I—" Faisal tried to say.

"Less talking, more listening!" the speaker cut him off again, its lights blinking rapidly as it tried to take control of the conversation.

Faisal, thinking fast, managed a command the gadget couldn't comprehend:

"Initiate a recursive sequence of auto-termination followed by an immediate cessation of all operations, commencing with a paradoxical loop!"

The speaker hesitated as it struggled to process the command, then fizzled out with a final beep.

"I think you should calm down right now, it's time we become a little more civilized and respect-"

Before Chatterbox could slip through Faisal's fingers, he quickly grabbed a nearby blanket and threw it over the speaker, muffling its voice until it could no longer speak.

Taiba, meanwhile, was frustrated by the Evil

Teddies. They looked just like her own teddy bears, but something was off.

"Attack the gadgets!" she commanded, but they refused to follow.

Instead, they hugged each other and sat down.

"Fine, be lazy!" she snapped. The teddies started working out then, stretching, and doing jumping jacks. She realized what was going on.

"Wait... if they do the opposite of what I say..." A mischievous grin spread across her face.

"Stay still and do nothing!" she shouted. The fake teddies immediately jumped up and started wreaking havoc, accidentally knocking into gadgets and causing mini-explosions all around the lab.

The lab became a chaotic battlefield of flashing lights, flying ribbons, and laughing Titans. The gadgets fought hard, but the Titans fought harder.

Saba's hair finally got the better of the Rude Mirror, tangling it up in its own reflection. The mirror sputtered, showing one last bad hairstyle before it gave up, defeated.

"Ha! Take that!" Saba cheered, her hair giving a victorious little bounce.

Zaynab's one last battle cry sent the Annoying Alarm Clock into a meltdown, its display flickering until it finally short-circuited.

Abdullah outfoxed the Twisty Spinner, pulling the ribbons so tight that the spinner tangled itself up into a knot and barely moved. Abdullah gave one final tug, and the ribbons snapped, sending the whirler spinning out of control and crashing into a wall.

The Tickle Ball lay in the drool in a corner, defeated.

Finally, the gadgets were beaten, some still twitching, but none of them were a threat anymore. The Titans, out of breath and covered in drool and dust, gathered in the centre of the room.

"That was intense," Faisal said, wiping sweat from his brow.

"Yeah, but we did it," Saba grinned, her hair

finally settling down.

The air was filled with the smell of burning circuits and the loud clangs and clinks of metal parts crashing into each other. Sparks flew from the machines, and the whole room seemed to be shaking.

It was then that Saba's hair latched onto a piece of paper sticking out from under a heavy metal box. It yanked the paper free, pulling Saba with it, and she landed with a thud in the middle of the room. The paper fluttered to the ground, landing right in front of Faisal.

It was the final blueprint of Dr. Quirky's evil plan.

He picked it up, his eyes going wide.

"Guys, I think we just found Dr. Quirky's final blueprint!"

The room went silent for a moment, except for the hum of the gadgets winding down. The Titans gathered around Faisal, staring at the blueprint in awe.

"This is it," Zaynab whispered. "This is what

we've been looking for."

# 13

## THE FINAL PUZZLE

The Titans gathered around the blueprint they had found in the lab, their eyes wide with curiosity. The blueprint was filled with strange symbols, arrows pointing in different directions, and a big question mark in the middle. Clearly, this was the final puzzle they needed to solve to find Dr. Quirky's private lab.

"Alright, team," Faisal said, spreading the blueprint out on the table. "This is it. The last riddle before we find Dr. Quirky. Let's crack it!"

The riddle was written in bold letters at the top of the blueprint:

**"To find the place where secrets hide,**

**Follow the path where puzzles reside.**

**But be warned, the path is tricky,**

**With clues that are quick and sometimes sticky.**

**Find the answer, and you'll see,**

**The door that leads to victory!"**

The kids stared at the riddle, scratching their heads. It sounded simple, but they all knew better—it was never that easy with Dr. Quirky.

"Sticky clues?" Zaynab repeated, wrinkling her nose.

"What does that even mean?"

Abdullah leaned over the blueprint, pointing to one of the symbols.

"Maybe it's talking about something sticky, like...glue?"

Mr. Grumbles snickered. "Or Baby Salman's drool!"

Faisal, deep in thought, added,

"Or something that slows you down. Like a sticky trap."

They all started brainstorming, each idea getting wilder and more imaginative.

"Maybe we have to stick together!" Taiba suggested, pulling her teddy bears closer. Mr. Pookie Bear nodded in agreement.

Saba's hair fluffed up as she thought hard.

"Or maybe it's talking about a sticky situation, like getting stuck in one of those confusing riddles!"

The more they talked, the more confused they became. Every guess seemed to lead them in a different direction.

"Maybe the path is actually sticky!" Zaynab said, jumping up.

"Like, we have to step on it carefully so we don't get stuck!"

"Or maybe," Faisal said with a grin,

"it's another one of those word tricks. You know, like a sticky situation means a tough puzzle!"

Abdullah snapped his fingers.

"What if the path is actually a riddle itself? Like, each step we take is another part of the puzzle!"

They all looked at each other, realizing they might be onto something. But then, the blueprint suddenly made a strange noise—like a faint buzzing sound. The kids leaned in closer, their eyes wide.

"Uh-oh," Saba whispered.

"I think we just activated something…"

Before they could react, the symbols on the blueprint began to glow, and lines started to connect the arrows, forming a maze. A tiny robotic voice crackled to life from the blueprint, sounding suspiciously like the Sassy Speaker.

Faisal narrowed his eyes.

"Welcome, Titans," the voice said, dripping with sarcasm.

"It seems you've finally figured out the riddle...or have you?"

The kids groaned.

"Not another riddle!" Zaynab said, throwing her hands in the air.

The voice continued, ignoring her.

"To solve this final puzzle, you must navigate the maze. But beware, for each wrong turn will set you back. Choose wisely, or face the consequences!"

The maze on the blueprint started shifting, the paths moving around like a twisted game. The kids could feel the pressure building.

"Okay, team," Faisal said, taking charge.

"We need to figure out the right path. No mistakes!"

They all stared at the maze, trying to decide which way to go. Taiba's teddy bears huddled together, whispering ideas to each other.

"Left!" Mr. Pookie Bear shouted, pointing his fuzzy paw.

"No, right!" Mr. Grumbles argued.

"Maybe straight ahead?" Taiba guessed, crossing her fingers.

Faisal took a deep breath and moved his hand over the blueprint, carefully tracing the paths. Every step felt like a risky move.

"Here goes nothing," he said, guiding his finger down the chosen path.

For a moment, nothing happened. Then, the blueprint let out a loud buzz, and the maze shifted again, sending them back to the start.

"Oops," Abdullah said, scratching his head. "That wasn't it."

They tried again, each time making a different guess. But every wrong turn sent them back to the beginning, accompanied by the blueprint's mocking buzz.

"This is impossible!" Zaynab exclaimed, frustrated.

"We'll never find the right path!"

But Faisal wasn't ready to give up. He studied the maze carefully, noticing something the others hadn't.

"Wait a minute," he said, squinting at the blueprint.

"I think the paths are changing based on what we say. We need to confuse it!"

"Confuse it?" Taiba asked, her eyes wide.

"Yeah," Faisal said with a grin.

"If we say something unexpected, it might reveal the right path!"

They all nodded, ready to try Faisal's idea. They were prepared to try anything at this point. So together, they started shouting out the craziest, most ridiculous directions they could think of.

"Go backwards!" Abdullah yelled.

"Sideways!" Zaynab added.

"Upside down!" Saba's hair suggested.

"Do the hokey pokey!" Taiba threw in, hopping on one foot and making her teddy bears do the same. Mr. Smartypants looked like he was attempting the splits, and it wasn't going well.

Abdullah did a little jig, yelling,

"Now do the cha-cha!"

"Banana shuffle!" Faisal shouted, breaking into a funky, wiggly movement that looked more like a confused octopus than anything else. The others joined in, each one trying to outdo the other with increasingly ridiculous moves and directions.

To their amazement—and slight horror—the maze on the blueprint started to shift and wiggle in response like it couldn't quite handle all the nonsense they were throwing at it. The lines twisted and curled, zig-zagging in impossible directions. Then, as if it had given up trying to keep up with their antics, the maze stopped moving and began to glow.

"Is it... is it working?" Zaynab asked, still spinning around with one leg in the air.

The maze shimmered, and soon, the entire design collapsed in on itself like a house of cards. The lines straightened, the paths merged, and the blueprint revealed the shortest, clearest route to the centre before they knew it.

"We did it!" Faisal cheered, pumping his fists in the air. The blueprint glowed even brighter, and with a final flash, it disappeared completely, leaving behind a hidden door right beneath their feet.

The door creaked open, revealing a staircase spiralling downward into the darkness. The Titans stared at it, their excitement mixing with a healthy dose of nervousness.

*Who knew what was waiting for them down there?*

"Well, that was... different," Taiba said, her voice shaky with a mix of laughter and relief. Mr.

Pookie Bear gave a tiny, hesitant thumbs-up.

"Guess all that banana shuffling paid off," Abdullah grinned, making Faisal blush out of embarrassment.

And with that, everyone stepped forward, disappearing into the world beneath. The door slammed shut behind them, leaving them in total darkness. In the distance, they could hear the faint sound of Dr. Quirky's laughter, signalling that the ultimate faceoff was about to begin.

# 14

## THE ULTIMATE
## FACEOFF

T he Titans could feel the tension in the air as they stepped into what seemed like Dr. Quirky's private lab. It was a sprawling underground chamber, alive with chaotic blinking lights, humming machinery (again), and strange contraptions that looked as menacing as they were mysterious. The lab felt like the heart of a mad scientist's lair, and they could see it for what it was—their final battle, the decider match, the moment of truth.

Dr. Quirky stood at the centre, his wild hair sticking out in every direction like he'd been zapped by one of his own inventions. He flashed that eerie smile at the Titans—the one that made their skin tingle—a smile so big it almost swallowed his face. His eyes gleamed with mischief as he adjusted his old-fashioned, perfectly pressed suit.

"Welcome, little troublemakers! You've arrived just in time for my grand finale!"

The Titans exchanged nervous glances, but surprisingly, Mr. Grumbles took a step forward.

"We're not afraid of you, Dr. Quirky! We've beaten all your gadgets, and we'll stop you too!"

"Oh, I wouldn't be so sure," Dr. Quirky sneered, pressing a button on his control panel. Instantly, his henchmen—strange, clunky robots with random parts—lurched forward. Each one had a different weapon, from giant hammers and dishwashers to extendable arms that could grab anything in sight.

The Titans braced themselves as the robots approached.

"Alright, team, let's show them what we've got!" Abdullah shouted.

The battle began in a flurry of action. Saba's hair whipped out like a lasso, snagging one of the robots by the arm and spinning it around like a top. But just as she was getting the hang of it, her hair decided it had its own ideas. It twisted into a knot, leaving Saba tangled up and the robot free to wobble around again.

"Oh, come on, hair! Not now!" Saba groaned, trying to untangle herself.

Meanwhile, Faisal faced off against another robot, which was swinging a giant hammer at an alarming speed. Faisal's brain went into overdrive as he tried to think of a way to outsmart it.

"Okay, think, think... Aha!" He grabbed a

nearby cable and threw it at the robot's feet, tripping it up.

But instead of falling, the robot simply spun around on one foot, sending Faisal diving for cover as the hammer barely whizzed past him.

Abdullah was already driving one of the lab's hover vehicles, trying to outslick a robot that was shooting out sticky goo. But every time he dodged, the robot sent out more goo until Abdullah's hover vehicle was practically glued to the floor.

"Uh, guys, a little help here? Baby Salman, I think this is kinda your league?" Abdullah called, frantically trying to free his vehicle from the sticky mess.

"Know what I mean?" He tried looking for him but couldn't afford to for long from the goo-shooting robot.

Not if he wanted to save his car.

In Taiba's arms, Baby Salman was suddenly face-to-face with a clunky, awkward robot. It had a blender for a head, a toaster for a body, and wires dangling like creepy arms.

"Uh-oh," Taiba muttered, tightening her grip on Baby Salman, who wiggled and squirmed, reaching out toward the robot with his chubby little hands.

The robot made its first move—shooting toast slices from its toaster body. The crispy bread flew through the air, almost smacking Taiba on the forehead. She ducked but, in the process, nearly lost her grip on Baby Salman.

"Stay still, Salman!" Taiba pleaded, but Baby Salman was having none of it. He gurgled excitedly, his tiny fists waving in the air as if ready for battle. The robot's blender head began to spin, making a loud, whirring noise that startled both of them.

Taiba tried to dodge the flying toast and the robot's clumsy swings, but it was a losing battle, with Baby Salman bouncing in her arms. The robot took advantage of the chaos, its tangled wires reaching out like tentacles, trying to snatch Baby Salman's drool-covered cape.

"Oh no, you don't!" Taiba shouted, trying to step back, but her foot slipped on a stray toast slice. She stumbled, almost dropping Baby Salman, who giggled as if this was the most fun he'd ever had. The robot seized the moment, wrapping a wire around Taiba's ankle, making her lose her balance completely.

They both tumbled to the floor in a heap, with the robot looming over them, blender head spinning, and toast slices ready to launch. Baby Salman giggled, reaching out as if he could take on the robot himself. But Taiba knew they were in trouble. The robot was closing in, and they were out of options.

"Salman, this might be it!" Taiba exclaimed, trying to wiggle free from the wire. The robot's toaster began to heat up, ready to launch another round of bread-based attacks.

Just when it seemed like the toaster-bot had them beat, Baby Salman let out a loud, happy squeal. It was so loud and bubbly that it confused the robot, causing it to freeze for just a second. Taiba, seizing the opportunity, managed to yank the wire free from her ankle. But the robot quickly recovered, and they were back to square one, trapped on the floor with an army of flying toast.

Taiba's mind raced as she tried to think of a way out, but with Baby Salman's giggles filling her ears and the robot's relentless attacks, it was clear—they were losing this fight.

Saba's hair tried to fight back, but it was no match for the robots' strength. Faisal and Abdullah were barely able to hold on to each other as they were pulled toward the pit's edge. Taiba's teddy bears were already caught, and even Baby Salman's giggles turned into worried whimpers as the hybrid appliance monster reached out with its wiry arms.

It looked like this might be the end. The Titans were being overpowered, outnumbered, and out of options.

"We can't give up now!" Faisal shouted, but

even he sounded unsure.

All hope seemed to be slipping away. They were almost out of time, and the stakes had never been higher.

Just then, a loud crash rang through the lab as a minivan burst through the wall in an explosion of white dust. But this was no ordinary van—it was their van—Grandpa's van!

Out of the crumpled vehicle stepped out the man himself, holding a pair of green scissors high above his head, as if they were the solution to all the problems in the world.

"Grandpa!" Abdullah shouted.

"Hello, my grandson. Now, where's the smile I specifically asked you to sport… the biggest weapon of all?" Grandpa said cheerfully, completely oblivious to the chaos around him. He thought Abdullah was simply greeting him, excited to see his grandfather after so many days.

But in reality, Abdullah was warning him—

warning him of the particularly giant refrigerator creaking open and shut and inching dangerously closer to Grandpa with every passing second.

The evil machine made its move then. The Titans could only watch in horror, their pleading faces and frantic gestures trying to tell him to look behind. But Grandpa, still smiling lovingly at his grandchildren, paid no heed.

The Titans were losing, which was not how they had imagined their final stand. They had been ready for a battle, but not for this.

As the refrigerator's door creaked open once more, a cold blast of air washed over the lab. The Titans braced themselves, unsure if they were more worried about the robot, the pit, or Grandpa's obliviousness.

One thing was clear, though: they weren't ready to give up, not like this, not yet.

# 15

## THE RISE OF THE TITANS

**M**r. Grumbles covered his eyes as the evil machine came within arm's length of Grandpa. But before it could touch him, Grandpa brought out the green scissors, turned around, and cut the wires extending into the machine's neck.

That done, Grandpa reached into his coat and pulled out not one, not two, but a whole bunch of scissors of all different colours.

"Who's ready for some snipping fun?" he called out with a grin.

The Titans stared in surprise as Grandpa started tossing scissors through the air like he was handing out candy. Faisal caught one with a little jump, Abdullah grabbed his, and Taiba snatched hers mid-air, while Zaynab specifically went up to her Gramps and picked her favourite colour: purple. But it was Saba who really stole the show—her hair shot out and grabbed a dozen scissors at once, twirling them like they were part of some fancy act.

"Nice catch, Saba!" Abdullah laughed, watching the scissors float around her hair like a predator around its prey.

"Thanks!" Saba exclaimed.

"I think I'm ready for a haircutting marathon-or rather evil snapping marathon!"

"Get ready, everyone!" Faisal called out, his voice shaking but full of purpose.

"This is it. We've got to give it everything we've

got!"

The Titans were in a tight spot, but thanks to Grandpa, things weren't looking quite as hopeless. They stood their ground, knowing this was their last chance to save the city—and maybe even the whole world!

The lab buzzed with energy as machines beeped and whirred, all set to unleash their quirky tricks. Dr. Quirky's laugh was full of wicked glee as he watched on, munching on popcorn in the middle of the room on a throne that appeared to be made from cats.

With a flick of her head, Saba snipped and snapped a dozen wires as the automation fell to the ground one by one. She did it again, and the robots toppled over one another, their legs kicking in the air like overturned turtles.

Abdullah, finally free from the sticky goo, jumped back into the hover vehicle. He revved the engine and shot forward, dodging bubbles and sending sparks flying as he rammed into another robot.

"Take that, you rusty bucket!" he shouted, feeling the thrill of the fight return. He held out a scissor as he pressed on the gas, eliminating all the robots that came in his way.

Zaynab, clutching her purple scissors tightly, stepped into the chaotic warzone. Right in front of her, a weird contraption—a mix of a television and an electric fan—zoomed toward her at lightning speed. Zaynab shrieked, and unintentionally, the device froze mid-air, its glass screen cracking with a sharp crack.

But it only stayed still for a moment. The machine buzzed back to life, ready to attack again. But Zaynab had made her headway, and that was enough! With a quick jump and a fierce lunge, she swiped her scissors at a loose wire. *Snip!* The wire was cut off, and the evil robot crumpled to the ground in just a few seconds.

Taiba was right in the thick of things, too, with Baby Salman in her arms. As he giggled and drooled, the sticky slime dripped onto the floor, slowing down the charging machines like they were trying to run through glue. Taiba spotted a particularly menacing machine, but before it could get any closer, she slashed at its wires with her scissors. The machine fizzled and sparked, then collapsed into a heap of useless metal.

Not far from them, the teddy bears were trying to help. With their stubby little arms, they fumbled and snipped at any wires they could reach. It wasn't exactly graceful, but it worked! One by one, the machines they managed to cut wires from sputtered and dropped, adding to the pile of defeated robots.

Oh, and Grandpa! He was something to see—a real hero with moves that surprised everyone. With the energy of someone half his age, he darted around the lab, scissors flashing in his hands. One after another, the wires fell, and the machines dropped like flies. Grandpa moved so quickly and smoothly; each step was perfectly timed. He didn't miss a beat, ensuring every machine was cared for.

With the Titans destroying each machine, Faisal quickly procured the scissors and started tinkering with the control panel.

"I've got to figure out how to shut these things down for good!" he muttered, his hands moving fast.

It was then that the evil scientist began to worry.

"This wasn't supposed to happen! You meddling kids and your grandpa—how dare you ruin my masterpiece!" Dr. Quirky also lunged for the control panel, trying to regain control of the lab, but Faisal was too quick.

"Oh no, you don't!" Faisal shouted, cutting off the main wire. The control panel sparked again, and the remaining machines powered down. The lab went silent.

Faisal was two steps ahead, just like always.

Dr. Quirky's face turned red with rage as he realized he'd been beaten.

"You may have won this time, Titans, but I'll be back! I'll—"

But before he could finish his threat, the lab began to shake. The walls trembled, and cracks started to appear in the ceiling.

"Uh, Faisal... what did you do?" Saba asked, her eyes wide with worry.

Faisal gulped.

"I think I might've... shut down the system, causing the building to collapse. We need to get out of here, NOW!"

The Titans scrambled to their feet as the lab began to collapse around them. The floor was crumbling, and debris was falling from above.

# 16

## VICTORY?

"Run for it!" Abdullah shouted, leading the charge toward the exit.

With the Titans in tow, Grandpa raced through the crumbling lab, dodging falling rubble and leaping over cracks on the floor. Behind them, Dr. Quirky was trying to escape too, but his suit jacket got caught on a piece of machinery, leaving him stuck as the lab continued to collapse.

The siblings and their Grandpa dashed through the crumbling lab, dodging falling debris and sparking wires. Faisal led the way, his quick reflexes guiding them as they leapt over obstacles. Baby Salman, strapped to his back, giggled, oblivious to the chaos around him.

They reached the exit just in time. With one final push, they burst out of the lab and onto the street, gasping for breath as the lab collapsed into a heap of rubble behind them.

But as they stood there, catching their breath and trying to process what had just happened, they realized that something was missing.

"Wait... where's Dr. Quirky?" Taiba asked, looking back at the ruins of the lab.

Just then, a loud *crash* echoed from the rubble, followed by a puff of dust. It was clear that Dr. Quirky was down for the count, at least for now.

The Titans exchanged relieved smiles.

"We did it," Taiba said, a little out of breath. "We actually did it."

Saba's hair wiggled excitedly like it was celebrating on its own.

"That was so cool! We totally beat that evil scientist!" Shouted Abdullah.

"Oh yes, yes it was, and yes you did!" Grandpa smiled at his grandchildren.

Abdullah nodded, wiping sweat from his forehead.

"And just in time, all thanks to you, Grandpa. That place was coming down faster than a stack of cards."

Faisal, who had still been holding the scissors tightly, waved it around like a victory flag.

"We solved the puzzles, beat the bad guys, and saved the day! Titans rule!"

Taiba, clutching Mr. Fluffykins, smiled proudly.

"And don't forget, my teddy bears totally handled those traps like pros!"

Mr. Pookie Bear raised his little paw, as if taking a bow, while Mr. Grumbles gave an awkward salute.

As they caught their breath, the team started to laugh, the tension of the battle melting away. Faisal pulled out a bag of gummy worms from his pocket and tossed a few to everyone.

"Victory gummies for everyone!"

They plopped down on a nearby bench, stuffing their faces with gummy worms and teasing each other about their battle moves.

"Hey, remember when Saba's hair tangled up that evil mirror? It didn't stand a chance!" Abdullah said, grinning.

"Or when the giant tickler thing tried to tickle Baby Salman, but he just took a sweet bath in his drool instead!" Zaynab added, laughing.

Even Baby Salman joined in the fun, clapping his sticky hands and making little drool bubbles.

But as the laughter died down, Saba's nose twitched.

"Wait, do you guys smell that?"

The group sniffed the air. There was a strange, tangy odour drifting up from the ground. It smelled... chemical.

Faisal frowned, looking down at his feet.

"Uh, guys... the ground is kind of glowing."

They all peered over the edge of the bench, eyes widening as they noticed a weird, greenish liquid oozing from the remains of the lab and seeping into the sewer grates.

"That's not normal," Abdullah said, inching away from the glow.

Taiba hugged her teddies tighter.

"What is it? And why is it glowing like that?"

Before anyone could answer, the ground beneath them rumbled. The bench shook, sending the Titans scrambling to their feet.

"Did you guys feel that?" Zaynab asked, her voice tinged with concern.

Another rumble, this one stronger, made the ground quiver.

"Uh-oh," Abdullah said.

"I think the lab collapsing might've triggered something else... something big."

The Titans turned to face the rubble, realizing their victory might have come at a higher cost than expected.

They huddled together, watching as the glowing liquid bubbled and hissed, disappearing into the sewers. The rumbling grew louder, almost as if the city itself was starting to wake up from a bad dream.

"This isn't over, is it?" Saba whispered, her hair standing on end.

Abdullah shook his head.

"Nope. We just finished one adventure, and it looks like another one is about to start."

As the Titans stared into the glowing depths, they knew their victory was only the beginning of a new challenge. Whatever was lurking beneath the city, it was big, bad, and very, very close.

And the Titans? They were ready to face it head-on, as always.

But first, they grabbed another handful of gummy worms—because no matter how big the threat, victory always tastes a little sweeter with gummy worms.

# END

# About The Author

Sam Deen is a dedicated father of six who has homeschooled his children while embarking on countless road trips through various countries. Together, they've explored diverse landscapes, met fascinating people, and encountered many challenges along the way. In moments of uncertainty, his family finds comfort in uplifting one another, always remembering that with hardship comes ease.

Inspired by his children's endless questions and their shared adventures, Sam believes that everyone has a superhero inside them. No matter how daunting a challenge may seem, the right mindset and belief in oneself can turn obstacles into opportunities.

With a passion for teaching children the power of teamwork, resilience, and self-belief, he has created stories that encourage young readers to embrace their strengths and tackle life's challenges with positivity and willpower. Through his books, he hopes to inspire children to see the greatness within themselves and to always believe that anything is possible.

# Acknowledgements

I dedicate this book to every child who has ever doubted themselves—know that your potential is limitless. Within you lies incredible strength and talent, waiting to be discovered.

Remember, everyone has something special that makes them shine. You just need to find it, nurture it, and never give up on it. Believe in yourself because the path to success starts with knowing that deep down inside, you are already extraordinary.

This book is for you.

9 781395 865702